AI Revolution: Decoding the Alchemy of Data

Horin

AI Revolution: Decoding the Alchemy of Data

Copyright © 2023 by Horin

The first edition was published in 2023

ISBN: 978-81-19747-87-0

Published by:
Ujwal
1663 Liberty Drive
Hyderabad, IN 47403
www.Ujwalublishers.com

Chapter 1: The Rise of Artificial Intelligence 07

The History of Artificial Intelligence

Understanding Artificial Intelligence

The Impact of AI on Society

Ethical Considerations in AI Development

Chapter 2: Unleashing the Power of Data   17

The Importance of Data in the AI Revolution

Data Collection and Storage

Data Processing and Analysis

Ensuring Data Privacy and Security

Chapter 3: The Alchemy of AI: Turning Data into Gold   25

The Fundamentals of AI Alchemy

Machine Learning and Deep Learning

Natural Language Processing

Computer Vision and Image Recognition

Chapter 4: Applications of AI Alchemy in Everyday Life 34

AI in Healthcare

AI in Education

AI in Finance

AI in Transportation

Chapter 5: Challenges and Opportunities in the Age of AI Alchemy 42

Job Displacement and Reskilling

Bias and Fairness in AI

Regulatory and Legal Implications of AI

Collaboration between Humans and AI

Chapter 6: Embracing the AI Revolution 50

The Future of AI Alchemy

Harnessing AI for Social Good

Building an AI-Ready Society

The Role of Education in the AI Era

Chapter 7: Decoding AI: Demystifying the Technical Jargon 58

Understanding AI Terminology

Popular AI Algorithms Explained

AI Tools and Platforms for Beginners

Resources for Further Learning about AI

Chapter 8: The Ethical Dimensions of AI 66

Ethical Considerations in AI Development

Transparency and Explainability in AI Systems

Ensuring AI Accountability and Responsibility

Establishing Ethical Guidelines for AI Deployment

Chapter 9: The Future of AI Alchemy: Predictions and Speculations 00

74

AI in Space Exploration

AI in Energy and Sustainability

AI in Entertainment and Gaming

AI in Personalized Medicine

Chapter 10: The Human-AI Partnership: Shaping a Collaborative Future   82

Augmenting Human Capabilities with AI

The Importance of Human Judgment in AI Decision-Making

Fostering Trust and Acceptance of AI

Coexistence and Collaboration in the Age of AI Alchemy

Conclusion: Embracing the Alchemy of Data in the AI Revolution   90

Chapter 1: The Rise of Artificial Intelligence

The History of Artificial Intelligence

In the Age of AI Alchemy, where data is transformed into gold, it is essential to understand the roots of artificial intelligence (AI) and how it has evolved over time. From its humble beginnings to the cutting-edge technologies of today, the history of AI is a fascinating journey that has shaped the world we live in.

The concept of AI can be traced back to antiquity, with mythical tales of statues and machines brought to life. However, the true birth of AI as a field of study began in the 1950s. During this time, scientists and researchers started exploring the idea of creating machines capable of human-like intelligence. The term "artificial intelligence" was coined by John McCarthy, who organized the Dartmouth Conference in 1956, widely considered the birthplace of AI.

In the following decades, AI research faced both breakthroughs and setbacks. Early AI systems showed promise in solving complex problems, such as playing chess or proving mathematical theorems. However, limitations in computing power and a lack of data hindered progress. The field entered a period known as the "AI winter," where enthusiasm waned, and funding for AI research diminished.

But in the 1990s, AI experienced a renaissance. Advances in computing power, the availability of large datasets, and innovative algorithms paved the way for significant breakthroughs. Machine learning, a subfield of AI that focuses on algorithms and statistical models, gained traction. This led to the development of practical applications like speech recognition, image classification, and recommender systems.

In recent years, AI has made remarkable strides. Deep learning, a subset of machine learning, has propelled AI into new frontiers. Inspired by the structure of the human brain, deep learning models called neural networks have achieved unprecedented accuracy in tasks such as natural language processing and computer vision. This has enabled the rise of AI-powered technologies like virtual assistants, autonomous vehicles, and personalized healthcare.

As AI continues to evolve, it is transforming various sectors of society. From finance to healthcare, education to entertainment, AI is reshaping the way we live, work, and interact. Its potential is boundless, with possibilities to solve global challenges, revolutionize industries, and enhance human capabilities.

In conclusion, the history of artificial intelligence is a testament to human ingenuity and our relentless pursuit of knowledge. From its humble beginnings to the present day, AI has come a long way. The Age of AI Alchemy is upon us, and understanding the history of AI is crucial for everyone. As we navigate this revolution, let us embrace the transformative power of AI and harness it for the betterment of all.

Understanding Artificial Intelligence

Artificial Intelligence (AI) has emerged as a groundbreaking technology that has the potential to revolutionize the way we live, work, and interact with the world around us. In this subchapter, we will delve into the depths of AI and unravel its mysteries, aiming to provide a comprehensive understanding of this transformative field.

At its core, AI refers to the development of computer systems that can perform tasks that typically require human intelligence. These tasks include speech recognition, problem-solving, decision-making, and even creative endeavors like painting or composing music. The key to AI lies in its ability to analyze vast amounts of data, learn from patterns, and make intelligent predictions or decisions based on that knowledge.

The age of AI alchemy has arrived, where data is transformed into gold. AI algorithms, powered by advanced machine learning techniques, enable computers to process and interpret the vast amounts of data generated in our digital world. This data-driven approach allows AI systems to continually refine their performance, learning from experience and adapting to new information.

AI has already made significant strides in various industries, including healthcare, finance, transportation, and entertainment. In healthcare, AI is being employed to assist in diagnosing diseases, developing personalized treatment plans, and improving patient care. In finance, AI algorithms are used to analyze market trends, automate trading, and enhance risk management strategies. Self-driving cars, virtual assistants, and recommendation systems are just a few examples of how AI is transforming transportation and entertainment.

However, understanding AI goes beyond its practical applications. It also raises important ethical and societal considerations. As AI systems become more sophisticated, questions arise about privacy, bias, and accountability. Exploring these issues is crucial to ensure that AI is developed and deployed in a way that benefits everyone and respects fundamental values.

In conclusion, this subchapter aims to provide a comprehensive overview of AI, its applications, and its impact on society. By understanding the core principles of AI, we can navigate the age of AI alchemy with confidence and harness its potential to improve our lives. Whether you are an expert or new to the field, this chapter will equip you with the knowledge needed to appreciate the power of AI and its transformative capabilities.

The Impact of AI on Society

In this rapidly evolving era of technological advancements, artificial intelligence (AI) has emerged as a game-changer, significantly influencing various aspects of our society. From healthcare and education to transportation and entertainment, the impact of AI is increasingly being felt across every sector. This subchapter aims to delve into the profound effects of AI on society, exploring both the opportunities and challenges that this revolution brings.

One of the most prominent areas where AI is transforming society is healthcare. With its ability to process vast amounts of medical data and detect patterns, AI has the potential to revolutionize diagnostics and treatment. From early disease detection to personalized medicine, AI algorithms are assisting doctors in making accurate diagnoses and recommending effective treatment plans. Moreover, AI-powered robotic surgeries are reducing the risk of human error and improving patient outcomes. However, concerns regarding the ethical implications of AI in healthcare, such as privacy and data security, must be carefully addressed.

In the realm of education, AI is reshaping the way we acquire knowledge and learn. Intelligent tutoring systems leverage AI algorithms to personalize learning experiences, adapting to the unique needs and pace of individual students. AI-powered virtual assistants are also becoming increasingly prevalent, providing instant answers to queries and assisting with administrative tasks. However, as AI takes on a more significant role in education, it is essential to maintain a balance between technology and human interaction, ensuring that students continue to develop critical thinking and social skills.

Transportation is another area profoundly impacted by AI. The rise of autonomous vehicles has the potential to revolutionize the way we travel, promising improved safety and efficiency on the roads. AI algorithms can predict traffic patterns, optimizing routes and reducing congestion. However, the widespread adoption of autonomous vehicles raises ethical questions, such as the decision-making process in critical situations. Striking the right balance between AI-driven innovation and ensuring human control is crucial in this domain.

The entertainment industry is also experiencing a significant impact from AI. Streaming platforms leverage AI algorithms to curate personalized recommendations for users, enhancing the viewing experience. AI-powered virtual reality and augmented reality are immersing audiences in interactive and immersive experiences. However, concerns regarding the potential biases in AI algorithms and their influence on creative expression and content consumption must be addressed to ensure a diverse and inclusive entertainment landscape.

In conclusion, the impact of AI on society is immense and far-reaching. From healthcare and education to transportation and entertainment, AI is transforming every aspect of our lives. While the benefits are undeniable, it is crucial to continuously evaluate and address the ethical implications and potential biases associated with AI. As we navigate the age of AI alchemy, striking a balance between technological advancements and the preservation of human values is essential to ensure a prosperous and inclusive future for everyone.

Ethical Considerations in AI Development

In the Age of AI Alchemy, where data has become the new gold, it is paramount that we address the ethical considerations surrounding the development of artificial intelligence (AI). As AI continues to permeate every aspect of our lives, from healthcare to finance, it is crucial that we understand the moral implications and strive for responsible AI development.

One of the primary ethical considerations in AI development is ensuring transparency. As AI algorithms become more complex, it becomes increasingly difficult to comprehend how decisions are made. This lack of transparency can lead to biased outputs and reinforce existing societal inequalities. To combat this, developers must prioritize transparency by designing AI systems that can explain their reasoning and decision-making processes. This transparency will not only enhance accountability but also foster trust between humans and AI.

Another crucial ethical consideration is privacy and data protection. AI systems rely heavily on vast amounts of personal data, and the misuse or mishandling of this data can have severe consequences. It is imperative that AI developers prioritize the protection of user privacy and adhere to strict data security measures. This includes obtaining informed consent, ensuring data anonymity, and implementing robust security protocols to prevent unauthorized access.

Fairness is another ethical consideration that must be addressed. AI systems should not perpetuate existing biases or discriminate against certain individuals or groups

Developers must be diligent in removing biases from training data and continuously monitor and evaluate AI systems for any unintended discriminatory impacts. Fairness should be a fundamental principle in AI development to ensure equal opportunities and outcomes for all.

Additionally, AI developers must consider the potential impact of AI on employment and human autonomy. While AI has the potential to revolutionize industries and streamline processes, it also poses a threat to certain job sectors. Developers must prioritize the responsible implementation of AI to minimize the negative impact on employment and ensure that humans maintain control over critical decision-making processes.

In conclusion, as we navigate the AI revolution, ethical considerations in AI development are of utmost importance. Transparency, privacy, fairness, and the impact on employment and human autonomy must be carefully considered. By addressing these ethical concerns, we can ensure that AI is developed responsibly, benefiting society as a whole while minimizing harm. It is our collective responsibility to shape the AI revolution in a way that aligns with our moral values and creates a positive and inclusive future for everyone.

Chapter 2: Unleashing the Power of Data

The Importance of Data in the AI Revolution

In the age of AI alchemy, where data holds the key to unlocking extraordinary possibilities, it is crucial to understand the importance of data in the AI revolution. Data is the lifeblood of artificial intelligence, acting as the fuel that powers the algorithms and models behind the transformative advancements we are witnessing today.

For everyone, from tech enthusiasts to business leaders, comprehending the significance of data in this revolution is essential. Data is no longer just a byproduct of our digital lives; it has become a precious resource, akin to gold. The AI revolution is about transforming this raw material into valuable insights, predictions, and solutions that can revolutionize industries, shape economies, and improve our lives.

Why is data so crucial? Simply put, AI algorithms need data to learn, adapt, and make accurate predictions. The more diverse and extensive the data, the better AI systems can understand patterns, recognize anomalies, and make informed decisions. Data fuels the machine learning algorithms that power AI systems, enabling them to extract meaningful information and generate valuable outcomes.

Consider the impact of data in healthcare. With access to vast amounts of medical records, genetic information, and real-time patient data, AI algorithms can identify patterns that humans may miss. This empowers doctors and researchers to make more accurate diagnoses, develop personalized treatment plans, and even predict potential health risks. In this context, data becomes the catalyst for medical breakthroughs and the driving force behind better healthcare outcomes.

The importance of data extends far beyond healthcare. In finance, for example, AI algorithms can analyze vast amounts of financial data to detect fraud, predict market trends, and optimize investment strategies. In transportation, data collected from sensors, GPS devices, and traffic cameras can be used to improve traffic flow, reduce accidents, and enhance public transportation systems. From retail to agriculture, every industry can benefit from the insights derived from data-driven AI applications.

In the AI revolution, data is not only valuable but also requires responsible handling. Ensuring the privacy, security, and ethical use of data are paramount concerns. As we navigate this transformative era, it is crucial to strike a balance between innovation and safeguarding individual rights.

In conclusion, data is the backbone of the AI revolution. Its importance cannot be overstated, as it allows AI systems to learn, adapt, and make accurate predictions. For everyone, understanding the significance of data in this revolution is key to unlocking its full potential. By embracing the power of data and harnessing it responsibly, we can pave the way for a future where AI alchemy transforms our world for the better.

Data Collection and Storage

In this digital era, where information is the new currency, the collection and storage of data have become crucial for individuals and organizations alike. With the advent of artificial intelligence (AI), the importance of data cannot be overstated. In this subchapter, we will delve into the intricacies of data collection and storage, exploring how it has transformed into a modern-day alchemy, capable of turning raw information into gold.

Data collection is the process of gathering and capturing information from various sources. In the age of AI, data collection has become more sophisticated and extensive than ever before. From social media platforms to smart devices and sensors, a vast amount of data is being generated every second. This data holds immense potential for understanding consumer behavior, predicting trends, and making informed decisions.

However, collecting data is just the beginning. The real challenge lies in storing and managing this vast trove of information. Effective data storage is essential for ensuring its accessibility, security, and usability. Traditional methods of data storage, such as hard drives and physical servers, are giving way to cloud-based solutions. Cloud storage offers scalability, flexibility, and cost-effectiveness, making it the preferred choice for businesses of all sizes.

But data storage is not just about finding a place to store data; it also involves organizing and structuring the information in a meaningful way. This is where data management systems and databases come into play. These systems enable efficient data retrieval, manipulation, and analysis. From relational databases to NoSQL solutions, there are various tools available to cater to different data storage and management needs.

Furthermore, data storage and collection must also be governed by strong ethical principles. As data becomes more valuable, the need for privacy and data protection becomes paramount. Individuals have the right to know how their data is being collected and used, and organizations must ensure that they comply with data protection regulations and best practices.

In conclusion, data collection and storage are the cornerstones of the AI revolution. The ability to gather, store, and manage data effectively can unlock valuable insights and opportunities. As technology advances, it is crucial for individuals and organizations to understand the importance of responsible data collection and storage practices. By harnessing the power of data alchemy, we can transform raw information into gold and pave the way for a future driven by AI.

Data Processing and Analysis

In the age of AI alchemy, the power of data cannot be underestimated. It has become the modern-day gold, holding immense potential to transform industries and revolutionize our lives. Welcome to the subchapter on "Data Processing and Analysis" from the book "AI Revolution: Decoding the Alchemy of Data."

Data processing and analysis are the fundamental pillars of extracting valuable insights from the vast amounts of information we generate every day. In this subchapter, we will delve into the intricacies of these processes, explore their significance, and understand how they contribute to unlocking the true potential of data.

Data processing involves the conversion of raw data into a more meaningful and usable form. It encompasses various steps, including data collection, cleaning, integration, and transformation. Data collection involves gathering data from diverse sources, such as sensors, social media, and transaction records. Cleaning the data ensures its reliability and removes any errors or inconsistencies. Integration merges different datasets to create a unified and comprehensive view of the information. Finally, data transformation prepares the data for analysis by applying mathematical, statistical, or computational techniques.

Once the data is processed, it is ready for analysis. Data analysis involves examining, inspecting, and transforming data to discover patterns, relationships, and insights. It utilizes various techniques, such as statistical analysis, machine learning, and data mining. Statistical analysis helps in understanding the significance of the data, identifying trends, and making predictions. Machine learning algorithms enable computers to learn from the data and make decisions or predictions without explicit programming. Data mining extracts valuable information from large datasets, uncovering hidden patterns and relationships.

The significance of data processing and analysis lies in their ability to turn raw data into actionable knowledge. They enable us to make informed decisions, identify new business opportunities, optimize processes, improve healthcare outcomes, and solve complex problems. The insights gained through data analysis can drive innovation, enhance efficiency, and fuel economic growth.

In the age of AI alchemy, data processing and analysis hold the key to unlocking the full potential of data. By harnessing the power of these processes, we can transform raw data into valuable insights, paving the way for a revolution in various industries and domains. So, whether you are an aspiring data scientist, a business professional, or simply curious about the world of data, understanding data processing and analysis is essential in the age of AI alchemy.

Ensuring Data Privacy and Security

In this digital age, where data has become the new gold, ensuring its privacy and security has become more critical than ever before. With the advent of artificial intelligence (AI) and its transformative capabilities, the need to protect sensitive information has become a top priority for individuals, organizations, and governments alike. This subchapter aims to shed light on the importance of data privacy and security in the age of AI alchemy, providing guidance for everyone in safeguarding their valuable information.

Data privacy refers to the protection of personal data from unauthorized access, use, or disclosure. With AI technology constantly evolving, it has become imperative to establish robust safeguards to protect individuals' sensitive information. Organizations must adopt stringent measures, such as encryption, authentication protocols, and access controls, to ensure data privacy throughout its lifecycle.

Furthermore, data security focuses on protecting data from unauthorized modification, destruction, or disruption. This involves implementing firewalls, intrusion detection systems, and other advanced security measures to safeguard against cyber threats. Regular security audits and vulnerability assessments should be conducted to identify potential weaknesses and address them promptly.

To ensure data privacy and security, individuals must also play an active role by practicing responsible data handling. This includes being cautious while sharing personal information online, regularly updating passwords, and being mindful of phishing attempts. It is important to educate oneself about the potential risks and best practices for data protection to mitigate the chances of falling victim to cybercrime.

Governments and regulatory bodies also have a crucial role to play in ensuring data privacy and security. They must enact and enforce stringent legislations and policies to hold organizations accountable for any mishandling of personal data. Data protection frameworks, such as the General Data Protection Regulation (GDPR), provide guidelines for organizations and give individuals greater control over their personal information.

In conclusion, data privacy and security are essential components of the AI revolution. With the alchemy of data transforming our world, everyone must understand the significance of safeguarding their valuable information. Organizations, individuals, and governments must work together to establish robust measures and frameworks that prioritize data privacy and security. By doing so, we can harness the power of AI while ensuring that our personal information remains protected from any potential threats.

Chapter 3: The Alchemy of AI: Turning Data into Gold

The Fundamentals of AI Alchemy

In this subchapter, we delve into the captivating world of AI alchemy, where data is transformed into gold. The age of AI alchemy has dawned upon us, revolutionizing every aspect of our lives. From healthcare to finance, education to entertainment, AI has become an integral part of our daily existence. But what exactly is AI alchemy, and how does it work?

At its core, AI alchemy is the process of using artificial intelligence to extract valuable insights and predictions from vast amounts of data. It combines the power of machine learning, data analytics, and advanced algorithms to unlock the hidden potential of information. By harnessing the immense computational capabilities of AI, we can discern patterns, make accurate predictions, and make well-informed decisions that were once unimaginable.

To understand the fundamentals of AI alchemy, one must first grasp the importance of data. Data is the raw material, the digital gold mine that fuels the alchemical process. Every interaction we have with technology generates data, creating an endless stream of information that holds the key to unlocking new possibilities. The more diverse and voluminous the data, the richer the insights we can extract.

The next fundamental aspect of AI alchemy is machine learning. Through machine learning algorithms, AI systems learn from the data, discovering patterns, and making predictions. This iterative process allows AI to continuously improve its performance and accuracy. By feeding the AI system with labeled data, it can recognize and classify new data points, providing us with valuable insights and predictions.

Data analytics forms another vital component of AI alchemy. It involves the extraction, transformation, and visualization of data to uncover meaningful patterns and trends. With the help of advanced analytics tools, we can identify correlations, anomalies, and outliers that might hold significant implications for decision-making.

Lastly, the algorithms used in AI alchemy play a crucial role in transforming data into gold. These algorithms are the secret recipes that enable AI systems to process and analyze vast amounts of data, uncovering valuable insights. From linear regression to neural networks, there are various algorithms that can be applied depending on the specific problem at hand.

In conclusion, the fundamentals of AI alchemy lie in the seamless integration of data, machine learning, data analytics, and advanced algorithms. Together, they form a powerful combination that has the potential to revolutionize industries, solve complex problems, and improve the quality of our lives. As we venture further into the age of AI alchemy, it is essential for everyone to understand its basics, as it shapes the very fabric of our technological future.

Machine Learning and Deep Learning

In this subchapter, we delve into the fascinating world of Machine Learning (ML) and Deep Learning (DL), two interconnected fields that are at the forefront of the AI revolution. These technologies have revolutionized the way we process and analyze vast amounts of data, enabling us to unlock hidden insights and make informed decisions like never before.

Machine Learning is a branch of AI that focuses on creating algorithms and models that allow computers to learn from data and improve their performance over time. It involves feeding data into a machine learning model, which then learns patterns and makes predictions or decisions without being explicitly programmed. ML algorithms can be broadly categorized into supervised, unsupervised, and reinforcement learning.

Supervised learning algorithms learn from labeled data, where the desired output is provided, enabling the model to make predictions or classify new, unseen data accurately. This approach is widely used in various applications, such as spam detection, image recognition, and recommendation systems.

Unsupervised learning, on the other hand, deals with unlabeled data, where the model identifies patterns, clusters, or associations within the data without any prior knowledge. This technique is particularly useful for tasks like customer segmentation, anomaly detection, and market basket analysis.

Reinforcement learning involves training an agent to interact with an environment and learn the best actions to maximize a reward. This approach has been successfully applied to autonomous vehicles, game playing, and robotics.

Deep Learning, a subset of ML, focuses on developing artificial neural networks inspired by the human brain's structure and functionality. These networks, known as deep neural networks, consist of multiple layers of interconnected nodes or neurons. Deep Learning has gained tremendous popularity due to its ability to automatically learn complex representations from raw data, such as images, speech, and text.

Deep Learning models, such as Convolutional Neural Networks (CNNs) and Recurrent Neural Networks (RNNs), have achieved remarkable breakthroughs in various domains, including computer vision, natural language processing, and speech recognition. They have enabled significant advancements in self-driving cars, virtual assistants, and medical image analysis, among others.

As we continue to generate enormous amounts of data, the synergy between Machine Learning and Deep Learning plays a crucial role in transforming this data into gold. The algorithms and models developed in these fields have the potential to uncover hidden patterns, predict future trends, and optimize processes across industries.

Whether you are an aspiring data scientist, a business professional, or simply curious about the AI revolution, understanding the fundamentals of Machine Learning and

Deep Learning will empower you to harness the potential of data and drive innovation in the age of AI alchemy.

Natural Language Processing

In the Age of AI Alchemy, one of the most fascinating and transformative fields is Natural Language Processing (NLP). NLP is a branch of artificial intelligence that focuses on the interaction between computers and human languages. It enables machines to understand, interpret, and generate human language in a way that was once thought to be purely the domain of human intelligence. With the advancement of NLP, we are witnessing a revolution in the way we interact with technology, opening up a world of possibilities for everyone.

At its core, NLP aims to bridge the gap between human language and machine language. It involves teaching machines to understand the intricacies of human communication, including grammar, semantics, and context. This enables machines to comprehend and respond to human language, whether it's in the form of written text, spoken words, or even gestures.

One of the key applications of NLP is machine translation. With the help of NLP algorithms, we can now automatically translate text from one language to another with remarkable accuracy. This has broken down language barriers and facilitated communication and knowledge exchange on a global scale. Moreover, NLP has also revolutionized the way we search for information. Search engines now utilize NLP techniques to understand the intent behind a user's query, providing more relevant and accurate search results.

Another exciting application of NLP is sentiment analysis. By analyzing text data, NLP algorithms can determine the sentiment or opinion expressed in a piece of text, whether it's positive, negative, or neutral. This has paved the way for sentiment analysis in social media monitoring, customer feedback analysis, and even stock market prediction.

NLP has also transformed the way we interact with virtual assistants and chatbots. By incorporating NLP capabilities, these AI-powered assistants can understand and respond to natural language queries, making them more intuitive and user-friendly. From booking a table at a restaurant to providing weather updates, virtual assistants have become an indispensable part of our daily lives.

As we delve deeper into the age of AI alchemy, NLP continues to evolve and push the boundaries of what is possible. It has become an essential tool in various industries, including healthcare, finance, and marketing. From medical diagnosis to fraud detection, NLP is transforming data into gold, unlocking valuable insights and driving innovation.

In conclusion, Natural Language Processing is a groundbreaking field that has revolutionized the way we interact with technology. It enables machines to understand and interpret human language, opening up a world of possibilities for everyone. From machine translation to sentiment analysis, NLP is transforming data into valuable insights, driving innovation in various industries. As we embrace the Age of AI Alchemy, NLP continues to push the boundaries of what is possible, creating a future where machines and humans can communicate seamlessly.

Computer Vision and Image Recognition

In the Age of AI Alchemy, one of the most fascinating and transformative fields is computer vision and image recognition. This cutting-edge technology has the power to analyze and understand visual data, unlocking a world of possibilities across various industries.

At its core, computer vision is the ability of a machine to interpret and understand visual information. It involves processing and analyzing images or video streams to extract meaningful insights. Image recognition, on the other hand, focuses on identifying and classifying objects within an image. Together, these technologies form the backbone of many AI applications we encounter in our daily lives.

One of the most impactful areas where computer vision and image recognition have revolutionized our lives is autonomous vehicles. Through a combination of sensors, cameras, and advanced algorithms, vehicles can now recognize traffic signs, pedestrians, and other vehicles on the road. This technology enhances road safety, reduces human errors, and paves the way for a future with self-driving cars.

Another significant application of computer vision and image recognition is in healthcare. Medical professionals can now leverage this technology to detect diseases and abnormalities from medical images, such as X-rays and MRIs, with remarkable accuracy. Early detection of diseases like cancer can save lives and ensure timely interventions.

Beyond healthcare and transportation, computer vision and image recognition have found their way into industries like retail, agriculture, and security. In retail, this technology enables personalized shopping experiences by analyzing customer behavior and preferences. In agriculture, computer vision can assess crop health, detect pests, and optimize farming practices. In security, it aids in surveillance by identifying suspicious activities or individuals.

However, the potential of computer vision and image recognition extends far beyond specific applications. This technology has the ability to analyze and understand visual content at a scale and speed that surpasses human capabilities. It allows us to unlock valuable insights from vast amounts of visual data, improving decision-making processes, and unleashing the true potential of data-driven strategies.

As we delve deeper into the Alchemy of Data, it becomes evident that computer vision and image recognition are integral components of the AI revolution. They hold the key to transforming raw visual data into valuable knowledge, empowering us to make informed decisions and shape a future where AI is seamlessly integrated into our lives.

In this subchapter, we will explore the fundamental concepts, algorithms, and real-world applications of computer vision and image recognition. We will unravel the mysteries behind object detection, image segmentation, and facial recognition. Get ready to embark on a journey that will open your eyes to the possibilities of computer vision and image recognition in the Age of AI Alchemy.

Chapter 4: Applications of AI Alchemy in Everyday Life

AI in Healthcare

In recent years, artificial intelligence (AI) has made significant strides in transforming various industries, and one area where its potential is truly remarkable is healthcare. The integration of AI into healthcare systems holds the promise of revolutionizing the way we diagnose, treat, and prevent diseases. From improving patient outcomes to streamlining administrative tasks, AI has the power to unlock a new era of healthcare that is more efficient, accurate, and personalized.

One of the key benefits of AI in healthcare lies in its ability to analyze vast amounts of data quickly and accurately. AI algorithms can sift through patient records, medical literature, and even genomic data to identify patterns and make predictions. This enables healthcare providers to develop more precise diagnoses and treatment plans, reducing errors and saving lives. Moreover, AI can assist in early detection of diseases by analyzing symptoms and data, leading to timely interventions that can significantly improve patient outcomes.

Another promising application of AI in healthcare is the development of virtual health assistants. These AI-powered virtual agents can provide personalized healthcare information, answer medical queries, and even offer recommendations based on individual health data. This technology not only empowers individuals to take charge of their health but also alleviates the burden on healthcare professionals, allowing them to focus on complex cases and providing more personalized care.

Furthermore, AI can help streamline administrative tasks, such as scheduling appointments, managing medical records, and processing insurance claims. By automating these processes, healthcare providers can reduce administrative costs, improve efficiency, and allocate more time to patient care.

However, the integration of AI in healthcare does come with its challenges. Ensuring patient privacy and data security is paramount, as the use of AI involves handling sensitive medical information. Additionally, it is crucial to address any potential biases in AI algorithms to ensure fair and equitable healthcare for all individuals.

As we enter the age of AI alchemy, the transformation of healthcare through the power of data and AI is inevitable. It is essential for healthcare professionals, policymakers, and individuals to understand the potential of AI in healthcare and embrace its benefits. By leveraging the capabilities of AI, we can unlock a new era of healthcare that is more efficient, accurate, and patient-centric. The future of healthcare is here, and AI is leading the way towards a healthier tomorrow.

AI in Education

In the Age of AI Alchemy, where data is transformed into gold, one area that has witnessed a remarkable transformation is education. Artificial Intelligence (AI) has emerged as a powerful tool in revolutionizing the way we learn, teach, and access educational resources. From personalized learning experiences to intelligent tutoring systems, AI has opened up new horizons for students, educators, and education providers alike.

AI has the potential to personalize education by understanding each student's unique learning style, preferences, and pace. With the help of machine learning algorithms, AI can analyze vast amounts of data to identify patterns and tailor educational content accordingly. This enables students to learn at their own pace, ensuring a deeper understanding of concepts and improved academic performance. Moreover, AI-powered virtual assistants can provide instant feedback and guidance, acting as personal tutors available 24/7.

In addition to personalization, AI has also transformed the way educators teach. AI algorithms can analyze student performance data to identify areas of improvement and suggest personalized teaching strategies. This allows teachers to focus on individual student needs and provide targeted support. AI can also automate administrative tasks, such as grading, thereby freeing up valuable time for educators to focus on actual teaching and mentoring.

AI has also revolutionized access to educational resources. With the advent of online learning platforms and Massive Open Online Courses (MOOCs), knowledge is no longer confined to traditional classrooms. AI algorithms can recommend relevant courses, tutorials, and resources based on individual interests, career goals, and existing knowledge. This democratization of education enables learners from all walks of life to access high-quality educational content and acquire new skills.

Furthermore, AI enables the creation of virtual and augmented reality learning experiences, providing students with immersive and interactive environments to explore complex concepts. This enhances engagement, promotes critical thinking, and fosters creativity.

However, as AI becomes more integrated into education, ethical considerations and responsible implementation become crucial. Issues such as data privacy, algorithm biases, and the role of human interaction in education need to be carefully addressed to ensure that AI is used ethically and responsibly.

In conclusion, AI in education has the potential to revolutionize the way we learn and teach. With personalized learning experiences, intelligent tutoring systems, and improved access to educational resources, AI is transforming education into a more inclusive, engaging, and effective process. As we navigate the Age of AI Alchemy, it is essential to embrace the opportunities and challenges that AI brings to education, ensuring that we harness its full potential while upholding ethical principles.

AI in Finance

In today's rapidly evolving digital landscape, artificial intelligence (AI) has become a game-changer across various industries. One sector that has seen significant transformation through the integration of AI is finance. AI technology has revolutionized the way financial institutions operate, enabling them to leverage the power of data and make more informed decisions.

The integration of AI in finance has ushered in a new era of efficiency and accuracy. With AI algorithms and machine learning models, financial institutions can process vast amounts of data in real-time, allowing for faster and more accurate risk assessments, fraud detection, and investment strategies. These capabilities have not only improved the overall customer experience but have also enhanced regulatory compliance and reduced operational costs.

One of the key applications of AI in finance is in the field of predictive analytics. By analyzing historical data and identifying patterns, AI algorithms can predict market trends, stock performance, and even customer behavior. This invaluable insight helps financial institutions make informed investment decisions, optimize their portfolio, and tailor personalized services for their customers.

Furthermore, AI-powered chatbots and virtual assistants have transformed customer interactions in the finance industry. These intelligent systems can understand customer queries, provide real-time support, and even execute transactions. This not only enhances customer satisfaction but also reduces the need for human intervention, resulting in cost savings for financial institutions.

Despite the numerous benefits AI brings to the finance industry, there are also challenges to consider. One major concern is the ethical use of AI in making financial decisions. As AI algorithms become more complex, it is important to ensure transparency and accountability in the decision-making process. Additionally, data privacy and security are paramount, as financial institutions handle sensitive information. Striking the right balance between innovation and responsible AI adoption is crucial for the long-term success of the finance industry.

In conclusion, AI has transformed the finance industry by unlocking the power of data. From improving risk assessments and fraud detection to enhancing customer interactions, AI has become an indispensable tool for financial institutions. However, it is essential to address ethical concerns and ensure data privacy and security in the age of AI alchemy. As we move forward, the integration of AI in finance will continue to shape the industry, providing innovative solutions and driving growth for financial institutions and customers alike.

AI in Transportation

Transportation is an integral part of our daily lives, connecting people and goods across the world. In recent years, the integration of artificial intelligence (AI) in transportation has revolutionized the industry, transforming the way we travel and transport goods. This subchapter explores the incredible advancements and potential of AI in transportation, delving into the alchemy of data that drives this transformative process.

AI has the power to optimize and enhance every aspect of transportation, from traffic management to vehicle automation. One of the most significant benefits of AI in transportation is its ability to improve traffic flow and reduce congestion. By analyzing vast amounts of data collected from various sources, such as traffic cameras, GPS systems, and weather forecasts, AI algorithms can predict traffic patterns and suggest optimized routes in real-time. This not only saves time and fuel but also reduces carbon emissions, making transportation more sustainable.

Moreover, AI plays a crucial role in vehicle automation, paving the way for self-driving cars, trucks, and even autonomous drones. These vehicles are equipped with advanced sensors and AI algorithms that enable them to perceive the environment, make decisions, and navigate safely. With AI technology, we are moving closer to a future where accidents caused by human error become a thing of the past. Self-driving vehicles also have the potential to revolutionize public transportation, making it more efficient, accessible, and affordable for everyone.

AI is also transforming the logistics and supply chain industry. By leveraging AI algorithms, companies can optimize their delivery routes, reduce costs, and improve customer satisfaction. AI-powered systems can analyze historical data on delivery routes, demand patterns, and other variables to predict optimal routes and delivery times. This not only increases efficiency but also enables companies to make data-driven decisions, ensuring timely deliveries and reducing waste.

In addition to optimizing transportation operations, AI is also improving safety and security measures. AI algorithms can monitor and analyze real-time data to detect anomalies, predict potential accidents, and alert drivers or authorities. Furthermore, AI-powered surveillance systems equipped with facial recognition technology can enhance security at airports, train stations, and other transportation hubs, ensuring safer journeys for everyone.

The integration of AI in transportation is transforming the industry, offering countless benefits to individuals and businesses alike. As we enter the age of AI alchemy, the ability to transform data into gold, the potential for innovation and advancement in transportation is limitless. By harnessing the power of AI and data, we can create a future where transportation is not only efficient and sustainable but also safe and accessible for everyone.

Chapter 5: Challenges and Opportunities in the Age of AI Alchemy

Job Displacement and Reskilling

In the Age of AI Alchemy, where data is transformed into gold, there is no denying that the rapid advancement of artificial intelligence has brought about significant changes in the job market. As we witness the rise of automation and machine learning, the fear of job displacement looms large in the minds of many. However, it is important to recognize that while AI may eliminate certain job roles, it also presents immense opportunities for reskilling and redefining our roles in the workforce.

Job displacement due to AI is not a new phenomenon. Throughout history, technological advancements have disrupted industries and rendered certain skills obsolete. However, what sets the AI revolution apart is the unprecedented speed and scale at which these changes are occurring. Jobs that were once considered secure and integral to our economy are now being automated, leading to concerns about unemployment and income inequality.

But amidst the challenges lies the potential for growth and transformation. As AI takes over mundane and repetitive tasks, it frees up human potential for more creative and complex roles. This shift necessitates reskilling and upskilling the workforce to meet the demands of the new economy. In fact, experts argue that reskilling is not just a response to job displacement, but also an essential strategy to thrive in the AI revolution.

Reskilling, however, goes beyond simply acquiring technical skills. It requires a mindset shift and a commitment to lifelong learning. In this age of constant technological evolution, the ability to adapt and learn new skills becomes paramount. It is crucial for individuals to embrace continuous learning and develop their cognitive abilities, critical thinking, creativity, and emotional intelligence.

Furthermore, governments, educational institutions, and organizations have a pivotal role to play in facilitating reskilling efforts. Creating accessible and affordable training programs, fostering collaboration between academia and industry, and promoting a culture of lifelong learning are all crucial steps to prepare the workforce for the challenges and opportunities of the AI revolution.

Ultimately, job displacement and reskilling are two sides of the same coin. While AI may disrupt traditional job roles, it also opens up new avenues for innovation and growth. By embracing the need for reskilling and adopting a proactive approach, individuals and societies can harness the power of AI to create a future where the alchemy of data truly transforms lives for the better.

Bias and Fairness in AI

In the Age of AI Alchemy, where data has become the new gold, it is crucial to discuss the pressing issue of bias and fairness in artificial intelligence (AI). As AI systems continue to infiltrate various aspects of our lives, it is paramount to ensure that these systems are fair and unbiased. This subchapter delves into the complexities surrounding bias in AI and the importance of fairness in the development and deployment of AI technologies.

AI algorithms are designed to learn from historical data, and if this data contains biases, the AI system is likely to perpetuate and amplify those biases. For example, if an AI system is trained on historical hiring data that exhibits gender bias, it may end up discriminating against certain genders in future hiring processes. This highlights the need to address biases in the training data and to actively work towards fair AI systems.

One of the challenges in achieving fairness in AI lies in defining what fairness actually means. Different stakeholders may have different perspectives on fairness, leading to ethical dilemmas. Should fairness be based on equal opportunity, equal outcomes, or something else entirely? These questions require careful consideration to strike the right balance.

Furthermore, biases in AI can have far-reaching consequences. Biased criminal justice algorithms, for instance, can disproportionately impact certain communities, perpetuating social injustices. It is imperative to develop frameworks and guidelines that ensure transparency, accountability, and fairness in the development and use of AI systems.

Addressing bias in AI requires a multi-faceted approach. It involves diversity and inclusivity in AI teams, as well as rigorous testing and evaluation of AI systems for potential biases. Ethical considerations should be embedded into the entire lifecycle of AI development, from data collection and algorithm design to deployment and ongoing monitoring.

To achieve fairness in AI, collaboration between experts, policymakers, and society at large is essential. Open discussions and public awareness campaigns can help educate individuals about the potential biases in AI and empower them to raise concerns. It is crucial to establish regulatory frameworks that hold AI developers accountable for creating fair and unbiased systems.

In conclusion, bias and fairness in AI are critical topics that demand our attention. As we navigate the AI revolution and transform data into gold, it is our collective responsibility to ensure that the alchemy of AI is guided by principles of fairness, equity, and transparency. By addressing bias in AI and striving for fairness, we can unlock the full potential of AI while minimizing the risks and pitfalls associated with biased systems.

Regulatory and Legal Implications of AI

As we delve deeper into the age of AI alchemy, where data is transformed into gold, it is crucial to understand the regulatory and legal implications that come hand in hand with this technological revolution. Artificial Intelligence (AI) has the potential to reshape industries and societies, but it also raises important questions regarding ethics, privacy, accountability, and liability.

One of the key concerns surrounding AI is data privacy. As AI systems rely heavily on vast amounts of data, there is a need to ensure that personal information is protected and handled responsibly. Governments and regulatory bodies worldwide are now grappling with the challenge of striking a balance between promoting innovation and safeguarding individuals' privacy rights. This has led to the introduction of regulations such as the European Union's General Data Protection Regulation (GDPR), which places strict rules on how organizations collect, process, and store personal data.

Another aspect of AI that requires attention is accountability. As AI systems become more autonomous and make decisions that impact individuals and society as a whole, questions arise about who should be held responsible for any negative outcomes. Traditional legal frameworks may struggle to assign liability when AI algorithms are involved. Therefore, new laws and regulations need to be developed to establish a clear chain of responsibility and ensure that those affected by AI systems can seek redress.

Moreover, the ethical implications of AI are gaining increasing attention. Issues such as algorithmic bias, discrimination, and transparency have become focal points for discussions. The decisions made by AI algorithms can have far-reaching consequences, from determining credit scores to influencing criminal sentencing. It is imperative to ensure that AI systems are fair, unbiased, and transparent, and that they do not perpetuate or exacerbate existing societal inequalities.

Furthermore, the rise of AI has also given rise to concerns regarding intellectual property rights. With AI's ability to generate creative works, questions arise about who owns the output of AI-generated content. As AI algorithms become more sophisticated, the line between human and machine creativity becomes blurred, necessitating a reevaluation of existing copyright laws and regulations.

In conclusion, the age of AI alchemy brings with it a range of regulatory and legal implications that must be carefully considered. Data privacy, accountability, ethics, and intellectual property rights are just a few of the areas that require attention in order to ensure that AI technology is harnessed for the greater good of society. It is essential for governments, organizations, and individuals to work together to establish a robust regulatory framework that promotes innovation while safeguarding the rights and well-being of all.

Collaboration between Humans and AI

In the age of AI alchemy, the transformative power of data is reshaping industries and revolutionizing the way we live and work. As we navigate this era, it is essential to understand the potential of collaboration between humans and AI. This subchapter delves into the intricate dynamics of this partnership, highlighting the symbiotic relationship that can be forged between us and the intelligent machines we create.

AI is not here to replace humans; instead, it is designed to augment our capabilities. By harnessing the immense processing power and analytical prowess of AI, we can unlock unimaginable insights from the vast amounts of data at our disposal. However, the true magic lies in the collaboration between humans and AI, where each brings their unique strengths to the table.

Humans possess creativity, intuition, and empathy—traits that are difficult to replicate in machines. We have the ability to ask the right questions, think critically, and make informed decisions. On the other hand, AI excels at processing massive datasets, identifying patterns, and performing repetitive tasks with unparalleled accuracy. By integrating these strengths, we can create a powerful alliance that transcends individual capabilities.

One of the most significant advantages of collaboration between humans and AI is the acceleration of innovation. AI algorithms can analyze vast amounts of data, spotting trends and anomalies that may elude human observers. By working together, we can uncover new possibilities, develop groundbreaking solutions, and drive progress in various fields, including healthcare, finance, transportation, and education.

Moreover, AI can act as a trusted advisor, offering data-driven insights to help humans make more informed decisions. From personalized recommendations and predictive analytics to risk assessments and fraud detection, AI can augment human decision-making processes, reducing errors and enhancing efficiency.

However, collaboration between humans and AI also poses challenges. Ethical considerations and concerns about privacy and bias must be carefully addressed. Transparent frameworks and regulations should be established to ensure responsible and fair use of AI technologies. Additionally, humans must remain at the helm, retaining control and accountability over AI systems, preventing them from becoming a black box.

In conclusion, the collaboration between humans and AI is a transformative force in the age of AI alchemy. By leveraging the strengths of both, we can unlock the true potential of data and drive innovation to unprecedented levels. This partnership has the power to revolutionize industries, improve lives, and shape the future of humanity. However, it is crucial to navigate this collaboration ethically and responsibly, ensuring that AI remains a tool in our hands, helping us decode the alchemy of data and turn it into gold.

Chapter 6: Embracing the AI Revolution

The Future of AI Alchemy

In the ever-evolving landscape of technology, the future holds a promise of unprecedented advancements. One such advancement that is poised to reshape the world as we know it is the field of AI alchemy. This subchapter delves into the possibilities and potential of this exciting frontier, as we explore the future of AI alchemy.

AI alchemy is the art and science of transforming data into gold. It is the process of extracting valuable insights, patterns, and knowledge from vast amounts of data using artificial intelligence. This transformative power has already begun to revolutionize industries and sectors across the globe, and its potential is only set to grow.

The future of AI alchemy holds immense opportunities for everyone, not just those working in the field of technology. With the increasing digitization of our world, data has become the new oil, and AI alchemy is the refinery that unlocks its true value. From healthcare to finance, education to manufacturing, every sector stands to benefit from the alchemical transformation of data.

Imagine a world where doctors can predict diseases before they manifest, thanks to AI algorithms analyzing vast amounts of patient data. Picture a future where autonomous vehicles navigate the streets seamlessly, making transportation safer and more efficient. Envision a reality where personalized education is tailored to each student's unique needs, fostering a love for learning.

The age of AI alchemy is not just about technological advancements; it is about empowering individuals and organizations to make better decisions, solve complex problems, and create innovative solutions. By harnessing the power of AI alchemy, we can unlock the hidden treasures within data, driving economic growth, and improving the quality of life for people worldwide.

However, as with any transformative technology, there are ethical considerations that must be addressed. The future of AI alchemy will require a careful balance between innovation and responsibility. As we embark on this journey, it is crucial to ensure transparency, accountability, and fairness in the use of AI algorithms. By doing so, we can mitigate potential risks and ensure that the benefits of AI alchemy are accessible to all.

In conclusion, the future of AI alchemy holds immense potential for everyone. It is a transformative force that will reshape industries, empower individuals, and drive innovation. However, it is essential to approach this future with a sense of responsibility, ensuring that AI alchemy benefits humanity as a whole. The age of AI alchemy is upon us, and it is up to us to navigate its path wisely, unlocking the true potential of data and transforming it into gold.

Harnessing AI for Social Good

In the age of artificial intelligence (AI) alchemy, where data is being transformed into gold, it is crucial to explore how AI can be harnessed for social good. AI has the potential to revolutionize various aspects of our lives, from healthcare and education to sustainability and social justice. This subchapter aims to shed light on the ways in which AI can be utilized for the betterment of society and create a positive impact on a global scale.

One of the key areas where AI can make a significant difference is in healthcare. AI algorithms can analyze vast amounts of medical data to detect patterns and provide accurate diagnoses. This can lead to early detection of diseases, personalized treatment plans, and improved patient outcomes. Moreover, AI-powered robots can assist in surgeries, reducing human error and increasing precision. By harnessing AI in healthcare, we can make healthcare more accessible, efficient, and cost-effective for everyone.

Education is another field that can benefit greatly from AI. Intelligent tutoring systems can personalize the learning experience, adapting to individual needs and abilities. AI can also assist in grading assignments and providing instant feedback, enhancing the learning process. Additionally, AI can help bridge the digital divide by providing access to quality education in underserved areas. By harnessing AI in education, we can empower individuals with knowledge and skills, enabling them to thrive in the digital era.

Sustainability and environmental conservation are pressing issues that require immediate attention. AI can be utilized to analyze large datasets and develop predictive models for climate change, deforestation, and pollution. This knowledge can inform policymakers and facilitate evidence-based decision-making. Furthermore, AI-powered systems can optimize energy consumption, reduce waste, and enable smart cities. By harnessing AI for sustainability, we can work towards a greener and more sustainable future.

Lastly, AI can play a crucial role in promoting social justice and equality. By analyzing historical data, AI algorithms can identify and mitigate bias in decision-making processes, such as hiring or lending. AI can also be used to detect and combat online hate speech and misinformation, fostering a safer digital environment. By harnessing AI for social justice, we can strive towards a more inclusive and equitable society.

In conclusion, AI has the potential to revolutionize various aspects of our lives and create a positive impact on a global scale. By harnessing AI for social good, we can improve healthcare, enhance education, promote sustainability, and foster social justice. It is crucial for policymakers, researchers, and technologists to collaborate and ensure that AI is developed and deployed in an ethical and responsible manner. Together, we can harness the power of AI to build a better world for everyone.

Building an AI-Ready Society

In this rapidly evolving digital era, the power and potential of artificial intelligence (AI) cannot be overstated. AI is revolutionizing industries, transforming the way we live, work, and interact. It has become the backbone of numerous technological advancements, enabling machines to learn, reason, and make decisions like humans. To fully harness the benefits of this AI revolution, it is crucial to build an AI-ready society that embraces and adapts to this transformative technology.

An AI-ready society is one that understands the potential of AI and actively prepares its citizens, industries, and governments to leverage its capabilities. The first step towards building an AI-ready society is education. It is essential to educate everyone, from students to professionals, about the basics of AI and its applications. By integrating AI education into school curriculums and offering training programs for adults, we can ensure that everyone has a foundational understanding of AI and its impact on their lives.

Apart from education, fostering innovation and collaboration is vital in an AI-ready society. Governments, industries, and research institutions must work together to create an environment that promotes AI research and development. This can be achieved by providing funding, infrastructure, and supportive policies that encourage the growth of AI startups and initiatives. By cultivating a culture of innovation, we can accelerate the pace of AI advancements and ensure that our society remains at the forefront of this transformative technology.

Moreover, an AI-ready society must address the ethical and social implications of AI. As AI becomes more prevalent, it is crucial to establish guidelines and regulations that govern its use. This includes ensuring transparency, accountability, and fairness in AI algorithms and decision-making processes. Additionally, we must address concerns surrounding job displacement and inequality that may arise due to AI adoption. By actively engaging in discussions and implementing measures to mitigate these challenges, we can build an inclusive and equitable AI-ready society.

Furthermore, an AI-ready society must prioritize data privacy and security. As AI relies heavily on data, it is imperative to establish robust data protection frameworks that safeguard individuals' privacy and prevent misuse of personal information. Strict regulations and standards for data collection, storage, and usage should be put in place to instill trust in AI systems.

In conclusion, building an AI-ready society requires a collective effort from individuals, industries, and governments. By investing in AI education, fostering innovation, addressing ethical concerns, and prioritizing data privacy, we can create a society that fully embraces and benefits from the AI revolution. The age of AI alchemy is upon us, and it is up to us to transform data into gold by building an AI-ready society.

The Role of Education in the AI Era

In the age of artificial intelligence (AI) revolution, education plays a pivotal role in shaping the future. As AI continues to transform various industries and revolutionize the way we live and work, it becomes imperative for everyone to understand its implications and acquire the necessary skills to thrive in this new era.

The AI revolution has brought about an unprecedented wave of technological advancements, enabling machines to perform tasks that were once exclusive to humans. From self-driving cars to virtual assistants, AI has the potential to reshape our world in ways we couldn't have imagined. However, its true potential can only be realized if we equip ourselves with the knowledge and skills to harness its power.

Education serves as the foundation for individuals to adapt and excel in the AI era. It is crucial for everyone, regardless of their age or background, to have a basic understanding of AI and its underlying principles. This knowledge not only fosters a sense of digital literacy but also empowers individuals to make informed decisions about their personal lives and careers.

Furthermore, education plays a critical role in addressing the ethical and societal implications of AI. As AI algorithms become increasingly sophisticated, it is essential to have a well-informed population that can critically evaluate the ethical implications of AI technologies. Educating individuals about the potential biases, privacy concerns, and impact on job markets can help create a more responsible and inclusive AI-powered society.

In addition to understanding the technical aspects of AI, education must focus on developing skills that are uniquely human. While AI can automate routine tasks, it cannot replicate qualities such as creativity, empathy, and critical thinking. Therefore, education should emphasize the cultivation of these skills, enabling individuals to adapt to the changing landscape of work and leverage AI as a tool for innovation.

To ensure that education meets the demands of the AI era, it is essential for institutions to adapt and evolve. This includes integrating AI into curricula, providing training programs for educators, and fostering partnerships with industry leaders. By doing so, educational institutions can equip individuals with the necessary skills to navigate the complexities of the AI-powered world.

In conclusion, education plays a pivotal role in the AI era by providing individuals with the knowledge, skills, and ethical understanding needed to thrive in an AI-powered society. It empowers individuals to make informed decisions, fosters the development of uniquely human skills, and ensures the responsible use of AI technologies. As we decode the alchemy of data and embark on the age of AI, education becomes the key to transforming data into golden opportunities for everyone.

Chapter 7: Decoding AI: Demystifying the Technical Jargon

Understanding AI Terminology

In the age of AI alchemy, where data is transformed into gold, it is essential for everyone to have a solid understanding of the terminology associated with Artificial Intelligence (AI). This subchapter aims to demystify the jargon and provide a comprehensive overview of the key AI terms that are shaping our world.

Artificial Intelligence, commonly referred to as AI, is a branch of computer science that deals with the development of intelligent machines capable of performing tasks that typically require human intelligence. It encompasses various subfields, including machine learning, natural language processing, computer vision, and robotics.

Machine Learning (ML) is a subset of AI that focuses on enabling systems to learn and improve from experience without being explicitly programmed. It involves algorithms that can analyze vast amounts of data, identify patterns, and make predictions or decisions based on that analysis.

Natural Language Processing (NLP) is a field of AI concerned with enabling computers to understand, interpret, and respond to human language. NLP techniques are used in applications such as chatbots, voice assistants, and language translation services.

Computer Vision is an area of AI that enables machines to understand and interpret visual information from images or videos. It involves tasks such as object recognition, image classification, and facial recognition.

Deep Learning is a subset of ML that uses artificial neural networks to model and solve complex problems. It is particularly effective in image and speech recognition, natural language understanding, and recommendation systems.

Neural Networks are computational models inspired by the structure and function of the human brain. They consist of interconnected nodes, or neurons, that process and transmit information. Neural networks are the backbone of deep learning algorithms.

Algorithm is a step-by-step procedure or set of rules followed by a computer to solve a problem or accomplish a specific task. In the context of AI, algorithms are crucial in training machine learning models and making predictions or decisions based on input data.

Big Data refers to large volumes of structured or unstructured data that cannot be easily processed or analyzed using traditional methods. AI algorithms thrive on big data, as they require substantial amounts of information to train and improve their performance.

By familiarizing ourselves with these AI terms, we can navigate the AI revolution with confidence and engage in meaningful discussions about its potential impact on society. As AI continues to transform industries and shape our lives, understanding these concepts will empower us to make informed decisions and embrace the opportunities that AI alchemy presents.

Popular AI Algorithms Explained

In this subchapter, we will dive into the exciting world of AI algorithms and explore some of the most popular ones used in the Age of AI Alchemy. These algorithms play a crucial role in transforming raw data into valuable insights, making them a fundamental part of the AI revolution. Whether you are an aspiring data scientist or simply curious about the inner workings of AI, this section will provide you with a grasp of the algorithms at the heart of this transformative technology.

1.   Linear   Regression: Linear regression is among the most fundamental algorithms used in AI. It aims to establish a linear relationship between input variables and a target variable. By analyzing the data, it predicts continuous outcomes, helping us understand how one variable affects another. This algorithm finds applications in various fields, such as predicting housing prices or estimating sales figures.

2.   Decision   Trees: Decision trees are intuitive algorithms that resemble a flowchart, making them easily interpretable. They partition the data based on various attributes, creating a tree-like structure for decision-making. Decision trees are widely used in classification tasks, such as spam filtering or medical diagnosis, as they provide clear insights into the decision-making process.

3.   Neural   Networks: Neural networks, inspired by the human brain, are complex algorithms capable of learning from vast amounts of data. Composed of interconnected nodes or artificial neurons,

neural networks can identify patterns and relationships in data, even when they are not explicitly defined. They excel in tasks like image recognition, natural language processing, and voice recognition, making them essential in today's AI applications.

4. Support Vector Machines (SVM): SVM is a powerful algorithm for both classification and regression tasks. It separates data into different classes by finding a hyperplane with the maximum margin between them. SVMs are versatile and can handle complex datasets, allowing them to solve problems like text categorization or stock market prediction.

5. K-Means Clustering: K-means clustering is an unsupervised learning algorithm that groups similar data points together. It partitions the data into a predetermined number of clusters, making it useful for customer segmentation, anomaly detection, or image compression. By identifying hidden patterns and structures within the data, K-means clustering provides valuable insights for decision-making.

Understanding these popular AI algorithms is crucial for harnessing the power of the Age of AI Alchemy. By decoding the inner workings of these algorithms, you gain the ability to transform raw data into valuable insights. Whether you are a data scientist, a business professional, or simply someone interested in AI, this knowledge empowers you to leverage AI technology effectively and navigate the exciting AI revolution.

AI Tools and Platforms for Beginners

In the Age of AI Alchemy, where data holds the immense potential to transform into gold, it is essential for everyone to understand the tools and platforms available to harness the power of artificial intelligence. Whether you are a tech enthusiast, a business owner, or simply curious about the world of AI, this subchapter will guide you through the basics of AI tools and platforms and help you embark on your journey into this revolutionary field.

Artificial intelligence tools and platforms are designed to simplify the process of developing and deploying AI solutions. These tools enable beginners to leverage the power of AI without requiring extensive technical knowledge or coding expertise. They provide an accessible entry point into the world of AI, making it possible for anyone to explore and experiment with this transformative technology.

One of the most popular AI tools for beginners is TensorFlow. Developed by Google, TensorFlow is an open-source library that simplifies the creation of machine learning models. It offers a user-friendly interface and a wide range of pre-built algorithms, allowing users to quickly build and train their own AI models. TensorFlow is widely used in various industries, from healthcare to finance, and has a vibrant community that provides support and resources for beginners.

Another valuable AI tool is Microsoft Azure Machine Learning Studio. This cloud-based platform offers a drag-and-drop interface, eliminating the need for complex coding. With Azure Machine Learning Studio, beginners can easily create, test, and deploy machine learning models. The platform also provides a vast array of pre-built algorithms and templates, enabling users to jumpstart their AI projects with minimal effort.

For those interested in natural language processing and chatbots, Dialogflow by Google is a fantastic tool. It allows beginners to build conversational agents that can understand and respond to human language. Dialogflow provides a user-friendly interface to design and train chatbots, making it an excellent choice for those with little or no coding experience.

In addition to these specific tools, there are also comprehensive AI platforms like IBM Watson and Amazon AWS AI that offer a range of services, including machine learning, natural language processing, and computer vision. These platforms provide a suite of AI tools and resources, making it easier for beginners to explore different aspects of AI and build sophisticated applications.

As a beginner in the field of AI, these tools and platforms will serve as your gateway into the vast realm of artificial intelligence. With their user-friendly interfaces and pre-built algorithms, you can unleash your creativity and transform your ideas into AI-powered solutions. Embrace the power of AI tools and platforms, and join the AI revolution as it continues to decode the alchemy of data, turning it into gold for everyone.

Resources for Further Learning about AI

In this rapidly evolving Age of AI Alchemy, where data is transforming into gold, it is essential for everyone to stay informed and keep up with the latest advancements in the field of artificial intelligence (AI). Whether you are a student, a professional, or simply curious about the potential of AI, there are numerous resources available to help you dive deeper into this exciting realm.

Books: One of the most comprehensive ways to learn about AI is through books. There are many titles available that cater to different levels of expertise. For beginners, "Artificial Intelligence: A Modern Approach" by Stuart Russell and Peter Norvig provides a solid foundation. For more advanced readers, "Deep Learning" by Ian Goodfellow, Yoshua Bengio, and Aaron Courville delves into the intricacies of neural networks and deep learning.

Online Courses: The internet offers a wealth of online courses that can help you understand AI concepts and develop practical skills. Platforms like Coursera, edX, and Udacity offer courses ranging from introductory AI to specialized topics like natural language processing and computer vision. The "AI for Everyone" course on Coursera, taught by AI pioneer Andrew Ng, is an excellent starting point for those with little or no technical background.

Podcasts: If you prefer to learn on-the-go, podcasts can be a valuable resource. "The AI Alignment Podcast" by the Future of Life Institute explores the broader implications of AI, while "Data Skeptic" hosted by Kyle Polich provides insights into various AI and data science topics. These podcasts offer a mix of interviews, discussions, and educational content to keep you engaged and informed.

Online Communities: Joining online communities can provide a platform for discussions, sharing ideas, and staying updated on AI trends. Reddit's r/MachineLearning and r/ArtificialIntelligence are popular forums where experts and enthusiasts engage in lively conversations. The Kaggle platform offers a collaborative environment for data scientists and machine learning practitioners to work on real-world problems and learn from each other.

Conferences and Meetups: Attending conferences and meetups is an excellent way to network with professionals and gain insights from industry leaders. Events like the International Conference on Machine Learning (ICML) and the Conference on Neural Information Processing Systems (NeurIPS) bring together researchers, practitioners, and policymakers, fostering a vibrant environment for knowledge exchange.

In conclusion, the field of AI offers immense potential, and staying informed is crucial to navigate this AI-driven world successfully. By exploring resources such as books, online courses, podcasts, online communities, and attending conferences, you can deepen your understanding of AI and unlock its transformative power. Embrace the AI revolution and embark on a lifelong journey of learning and discovery.

Chapter 8: The Ethical Dimensions of AI

Ethical Considerations in AI Development

In the age of AI alchemy, where data is transforming into gold, it becomes imperative to address the ethical considerations in AI development. Artificial Intelligence (AI) has the potential to revolutionize various aspects of our lives, from healthcare to transportation, but its development also raises ethical dilemmas that cannot be ignored.

One crucial ethical consideration is the potential for bias in AI algorithms. AI systems learn from vast amounts of data, and if that data contains bias, the AI can perpetuate and amplify these biases. This can result in unfair treatment or discrimination against certain individuals or groups. It is essential for developers to carefully curate and assess the data used to train AI models, ensuring that bias is minimized and fairness is prioritized.

Transparency in AI decision-making is another ethical concern. As AI systems become increasingly complex and autonomous, it becomes challenging to understand how they arrive at their conclusions. The lack of transparency can lead to mistrust and concerns about accountability. Developers must strive to make AI systems explainable, ensuring that they can provide understandable and justifiable explanations for their decisions.

Privacy and security are also key ethical considerations in AI development. AI systems often rely on vast amounts of personal data, which raises concerns about potential misuse or unauthorized access. Developers must incorporate robust privacy measures, such as anonymization and encryption, to protect individuals' sensitive information. Additionally, it is crucial to implement stringent security protocols to prevent malicious actors from exploiting AI systems for their own gain.

Another ethical consideration is the potential impact of AI on employment. While AI has the potential to improve efficiency and productivity, it also raises concerns about job displacement and the widening of socioeconomic inequalities. It is crucial for policymakers and organizations to address these concerns by investing in retraining programs and creating new job opportunities that complement AI technologies.

Lastly, ethical considerations should extend to the broader societal impacts of AI. Developers and policymakers must consider the potential consequences of AI deployment on social structures, power dynamics, and human rights. Ethical frameworks should be established to guide the responsible and equitable development and deployment of AI systems.

In conclusion, the age of AI alchemy presents immense opportunities, but it also demands careful ethical considerations in AI development. Addressing biases, ensuring transparency, safeguarding privacy and security, mitigating job displacement, and considering societal impacts are essential steps towards responsible AI development. By prioritizing ethics, we can harness the transformative power of AI while protecting the values and rights of individuals and society as a whole.

Transparency and Explainability in AI Systems

In the Age of AI Alchemy, where data is transforming into gold, the concept of transparency and explainability in AI systems becomes paramount. As AI algorithms become increasingly complex and omnipresent, it is crucial for everyone to understand how these systems work and why they make the decisions they do. This subchapter delves into the significance of transparency and explainability in AI, shedding light on the inner workings of these advanced technologies.

Transparency refers to the ability to clearly understand and trace the decision-making processes of AI models. It is about making AI systems more accessible and accountable to users, regulators, and society as a whole. With transparency, individuals can better comprehend how AI algorithms arrive at certain conclusions, ensuring fairness and promoting trust in these systems.

Explainability, on the other hand, goes beyond transparency by providing a detailed rationale for AI decisions. It involves the ability to explain the reasoning behind the outcomes produced by AI models in a way that is understandable to humans. By making AI explainable, we can mitigate biases, address ethical concerns, and enhance the overall trustworthiness of AI systems.

The demand for transparency and explainability arises from the increasing reliance on AI systems in various domains, ranging from finance and healthcare to criminal justice and autonomous vehicles. When an AI algorithm denies a loan application, diagnoses a disease, determines a prison sentence, or controls a self-driving car, it is essential for individuals to understand how and why these decisions were made. Without transparency and explainability, the potential risks and unintended consequences of AI systems can be significant.

To achieve transparency and explainability, researchers and developers are working towards developing new techniques and tools. Techniques such as interpretability algorithms, model-agnostic explanations, and rule-based systems are being explored to shed light on the inner workings of AI models. Additionally, regulations and standards are being developed to ensure the ethical and responsible use of AI in society.

Ultimately, transparency and explainability in AI systems are not only crucial for regulatory compliance but also for building trust and fostering wider acceptance of AI technologies. It is vital for everyone to understand the inner workings of AI algorithms, empowering individuals to question, challenge, and improve these systems. As we navigate the AI revolution, transparency and explainability pave the way for a future where AI is not a black box but a tool that enhances our lives while upholding ethical and societal values.

Ensuring AI Accountability and Responsibility

In this rapidly evolving Age of AI Alchemy, where data is being transformed into gold, it is crucial for us, as a society, to address the issues of AI accountability and responsibility. As artificial intelligence becomes more prevalent in our daily lives, it is imperative to ensure that AI systems are designed and implemented with ethical considerations in mind.

AI technologies have the potential to revolutionize various sectors, from healthcare and transportation to finance and entertainment. However, with great power comes great responsibility. We must take proactive measures to prevent the misuse or abuse of AI systems and algorithms.

One of the key aspects of ensuring AI accountability is transparency. Developers and organizations must be transparent about the data sources, algorithms, and decision-making processes behind AI systems. This transparency will help build trust between users and AI technologies, as well as enable users to understand and question the decisions made by AI systems.

Additionally, accountability in AI can be fostered through clear regulations and guidelines. Governments and regulatory bodies should work in collaboration with AI developers to establish frameworks that address the ethical implications of AI. These frameworks should include guidelines for data privacy, algorithmic bias, and the potential impact of AI on employment.

Furthermore, AI accountability can be enhanced through rigorous testing and validation processes. Before deploying

AI systems, they should be thoroughly tested for potential biases, errors, and vulnerabilities. Continuous monitoring and auditing of AI systems will help identify and rectify any issues that may arise.

Responsible AI development also requires diverse and inclusive teams. The development process should involve individuals from various backgrounds to ensure that AI systems are free from biases and prejudices. This diversity will help prevent the perpetuation of existing societal inequalities through AI technologies.

Lastly, education and awareness play a vital role in ensuring AI accountability. It is necessary to educate individuals about the capabilities and limitations of AI systems, as well as the ethical considerations surrounding their use. By raising awareness, we can collectively work towards a future where AI is developed and used responsibly.

In conclusion, in this Age of AI Alchemy, it is crucial to prioritize AI accountability and responsibility. Transparency, regulations, rigorous testing, diversity in development teams, and education are all vital components in ensuring that AI technologies are ethically developed and used. By addressing these aspects, we can harness the potential of AI while minimizing the risks and maximizing the benefits for everyone in society.

Establishing Ethical Guidelines for AI Deployment

In the Age of AI Alchemy, where data holds the key to unlocking untold potential, it is vital that we address the ethical implications of deploying artificial intelligence (AI) systems. As AI continues to revolutionize industries and shape our daily lives, we must establish robust guidelines to ensure its responsible and ethical deployment.

The rapid advancements in AI technology have the power to transform data into gold, but with great power comes great responsibility. AI algorithms have the potential to make decisions that affect individuals, communities, and even nations. It is imperative that we establish a framework of ethical guidelines to guide the development and deployment of AI systems.

One crucial aspect of ethical AI deployment is transparency. Users, consumers, and stakeholders should have a clear understanding of how AI systems work, the data used, and the decisions they make. Transparency helps build trust and ensures accountability, as it allows for scrutiny and evaluation of AI systems to prevent biases, discrimination, or unethical practices.

Another key consideration is fairness. AI systems should be developed and deployed in a manner that is fair and unbiased, ensuring equal opportunities and treatment for all individuals, regardless of their gender, race, or socioeconomic background. This requires careful consideration of the data used to train AI models, as biased or discriminatory data can perpetuate and amplify existing societal inequalities.

Privacy and data protection are also vital aspects of ethical AI deployment. As AI systems rely on vast amounts of data, it is crucial to handle and store this data securely, respecting individuals' rights to privacy. Robust data protection mechanisms and consent frameworks must be established to safeguard individuals' personal information and prevent misuse or unauthorized access.

Moreover, AI systems should be designed with a focus on safety and reliability. AI algorithms that control critical infrastructure, such as autonomous vehicles or healthcare systems, must be thoroughly tested and validated to ensure they operate safely and reliably, minimizing the potential for accidents or harm.

Finally, ongoing monitoring and evaluation of AI systems are essential to identify and address any ethical concerns that may arise during their deployment. Regular audits and assessments should be conducted to ensure compliance with ethical guidelines and to update them as technology evolves.

In conclusion, as we navigate the Age of AI Alchemy, establishing ethical guidelines for AI deployment is of utmost importance. Transparency, fairness, privacy, safety, and ongoing evaluation are key pillars that must be incorporated into the development and deployment of AI systems. By doing so, we can ensure that AI is harnessed for the benefit of all, transforming data into gold ethically and responsibly.

Chapter 9: The Future of AI Alchemy: Predictions and Speculations

AI in Space Exploration

In the Age of AI Alchemy, where data is transformed into gold, one field that has witnessed remarkable advancements is space exploration. The integration of artificial intelligence (AI) with space exploration has revolutionized our understanding of the cosmos and opened up unprecedented opportunities for scientific discovery. This subchapter delves into the awe-inspiring applications and implications of AI in space exploration.

From the moment humans first gazed at the stars, we have yearned to explore the vastness of space. Now, with the help of AI, we are able to venture further and deeper into the unknown. AI algorithms have been employed to analyze massive amounts of data collected by telescopes, satellites, and space probes. This has enabled astronomers and scientists to detect celestial objects with remarkable precision, identify exoplanets, and even unravel the mysteries of dark matter.

One of the key aspects of AI in space exploration is its ability to assist in autonomous decision-making. In the harsh and unpredictable environment of space, AI systems can ensure the safety and efficiency of missions. These intelligent systems can analyze real-time data, anticipate potential risks, and make split-second decisions to protect astronauts and equipment. With AI at the helm, space missions become more reliable, cost-effective, and capable of accomplishing complex tasks.

Furthermore, AI has facilitated the development of autonomous robots that can be deployed in space. These robots are equipped with advanced AI algorithms, enabling them to navigate treacherous terrain, collect samples, and conduct experiments. By removing the need for human intervention, these robots can explore distant planets and moons, providing valuable insights into their composition, geological features, and potential for sustaining life.

Another area where AI has made significant strides is in satellite imagery and Earth observation. AI algorithms can analyze vast amounts of satellite data to monitor climate change, predict natural disasters, and track the health of our planet. This information is invaluable for policymakers, scientists, and environmentalists, as it aids in making informed decisions and taking proactive measures to safeguard our environment.

In conclusion, AI has become a game-changer in the field of space exploration. Its integration with astronomical research, autonomous decision-making, and robotic exploration has revolutionized our understanding of the cosmos. By utilizing AI algorithms, we can analyze vast amounts of data with precision, enhance the safety and efficiency of missions, and unravel the mysteries of the universe. As we continue to unlock the alchemy of data, AI will undoubtedly propel us further into the depths of space, uncovering secrets that have remained hidden for eons.

AI in Energy and Sustainability

In today's rapidly evolving world, the importance of energy and sustainability cannot be overstated. As we strive to find ways to reduce our carbon footprint, minimize waste, and preserve our planet for future generations, the role of artificial intelligence (AI) becomes increasingly significant. AI has the potential to revolutionize the way we generate, distribute, and consume energy, offering innovative solutions that can address the pressing challenges of our time.

One area where AI is making a significant impact is in the optimization of energy generation and consumption. By leveraging machine learning algorithms, AI systems can analyze vast amounts of data and identify patterns that humans might overlook. This enables us to optimize energy production, ensuring that resources are used efficiently and that renewable sources are harnessed to their full potential. AI algorithms can predict energy demand, helping grid operators balance supply and demand in real-time, reducing wastage and improving overall efficiency.

Furthermore, AI can enhance the management and maintenance of energy infrastructure. By monitoring sensor data and using predictive analytics, AI-powered systems can identify potential faults or anomalies in power grids, enabling proactive repairs and minimizing downtime. This not only increases the reliability of energy distribution but also reduces costs and improves safety.

In the pursuit of sustainability, AI is also playing a pivotal role in optimizing resource utilization. By integrating AI into smart grids and energy management systems, we can reduce energy consumption in buildings, factories, and transportation. AI algorithms can analyze consumption patterns, identify energy-saving opportunities, and even control devices to optimize usage automatically. This not only reduces carbon emissions but also leads to significant cost savings for individuals and businesses.

Moreover, AI is driving breakthroughs in renewable energy technologies. Through AI-enabled simulations and modeling, researchers can design more efficient solar panels and wind turbines, improving their performance and increasing energy generation. AI algorithms can also optimize the placement of renewable energy infrastructure, identifying the most suitable locations for solar farms or wind turbines based on factors such as weather patterns and land availability.

In conclusion, the integration of AI in the energy and sustainability sectors is ushering in a new era of efficiency, cost-effectiveness, and environmental stewardship. By harnessing the power of data and machine learning algorithms, we can transform our energy systems, reduce waste, and mitigate the impact of climate change. The Age of AI Alchemy is truly transforming data into gold, paving the way for a sustainable future for everyone.

AI in Entertainment and Gaming

In the Age of AI Alchemy, where data is transformed into gold, the realm of entertainment and gaming stands as a shining example of how artificial intelligence (AI) is revolutionizing our lives. AI has become an integral part of our entertainment experiences, enhancing everything from movie recommendations to immersive gaming adventures.

One of the most significant ways AI is transforming entertainment is through personalized recommendations. Gone are the days of aimlessly scrolling through catalogs, unsure of what to watch or play next. AI algorithms now analyze our viewing and gaming habits, taking into account our preferences, genres, and even mood, to suggest content tailored to our individual tastes. These recommendations not only save time but also introduce us to new and exciting experiences we may have otherwise missed.

AI-powered virtual assistants have also made their presence felt in the world of entertainment. These intelligent companions, such as Siri, Alexa, and Google Assistant, can answer our questions, play our favorite songs, and even control our smart home devices, all with a simple voice command. As AI continues to advance, these virtual assistants are becoming even more intuitive, able to understand context and engage in natural conversations, making them indispensable companions for our entertainment needs.

In the gaming industry, AI has taken center stage, revolutionizing the way games are designed, played, and experienced. AI-powered algorithms can generate lifelike characters, realistic environments, and dynamic storylines, creating immersive gaming worlds that blur the line between reality and fantasy. Moreover, AI-driven game engines can adapt to players' behaviors, adjusting difficulty levels, and providing personalized challenges to ensure an engaging and rewarding experience for all gamers.

Furthermore, AI is not limited to enhancing the user experience; it also plays a vital role in improving game development processes. AI algorithms can analyze massive amounts of data, including player feedback, to identify trends, optimize gameplay mechanics, and even predict future gaming trends. This data-driven approach enables game developers to create more innovative and successful games, keeping players engaged and entertained.

As AI continues to evolve, the possibilities for its integration into entertainment and gaming are endless. From interactive virtual reality experiences to AI-generated content, the future promises even more exciting and immersive entertainment experiences. The Age of AI Alchemy has truly transformed entertainment and gaming, making them more accessible, enjoyable, and personalized for everyone. So, whether you're a movie enthusiast or a hardcore gamer, buckle up for an exhilarating journey into the world of AI-powered entertainment and gaming.

AI in Personalized Medicine

In the age of AI alchemy, where data is transformed into gold, one of the most exciting and transformative applications is in the field of personalized medicine. The convergence of artificial intelligence and healthcare is revolutionizing the way we diagnose, treat, and prevent diseases. This subchapter delves into the immense potential of AI in personalized medicine and its implications for everyone.

Personalized medicine is an approach that recognizes the unique characteristics of each individual and tailors medical treatments accordingly. With the advent of AI, this concept has been taken to new heights. AI algorithms can analyze vast amounts of patient data, including genetic information, medical records, lifestyle factors, and even social determinants of health. By identifying patterns and correlations in this wealth of data, AI can provide personalized insights and recommendations for patients.

One of the most significant contributions of AI in personalized medicine is in the field of diagnostics. AI algorithms can analyze medical images, such as X-rays, MRIs, and CT scans, with unparalleled accuracy. This enables early detection of diseases like cancer, allowing for timely intervention and improved patient outcomes. By combining image analysis with genetic data, AI can also predict an individual's risk of developing certain diseases, empowering proactive healthcare decisions.

Treatment planning is another area where AI is transforming personalized medicine. AI algorithms can analyze data from thousands of clinical trials, research papers, and patient records to identify the most effective treatment options for an individual's unique condition. This ensures that patients receive the most targeted and efficient treatments, minimizing adverse effects and optimizing therapeutic outcomes.

Furthermore, AI-powered virtual assistants and chatbots are revolutionizing the way patients interact with healthcare providers. These intelligent systems can provide personalized health advice, answer questions, and even monitor patients' vital signs remotely. This not only enhances patient engagement but also improves access to healthcare, especially for individuals in underserved areas.

However, the integration of AI in personalized medicine also raises ethical and privacy concerns. Safeguarding patient data, ensuring transparency in AI algorithms, and maintaining a human touch in healthcare delivery are crucial aspects that need to be addressed as we navigate this AI revolution.

In conclusion, AI in personalized medicine is a game-changer that holds immense promise for everyone. By harnessing the power of AI algorithms, healthcare practitioners can provide individualized care, leading to improved patient outcomes and a more efficient healthcare system. As we embrace the age of AI alchemy, it is essential to strike a balance between technological advancements and ethical considerations, ensuring that personalized medicine remains a human-centered pursuit.

Chapter 10: The Human-AI Partnership: Shaping a Collaborative Future

Augmenting Human Capabilities with AI

In the age of rapid technological advancements, Artificial Intelligence (AI) has emerged as a transformative force, reshaping industries and societies alike. With its ability to process vast amounts of data at lightning speed and learn from it, AI has become synonymous with the promise of unlocking human potential like never before. This subchapter explores the concept of augmenting human capabilities with AI, delving into the ways in which this revolutionary technology can enhance our abilities and empower us to achieve new heights.

AI, at its core, is not meant to replace humans but to collaborate with them. By leveraging AI algorithms and machine learning models, we can amplify our cognitive abilities and make more informed decisions. Whether it's in healthcare, education, finance, or any other field, AI has the potential to augment our skills, enabling us to accomplish tasks more efficiently and effectively.

One of the key strengths of AI lies in its ability to analyze massive amounts of complex data in real-time. This empowers professionals across various industries to make data-driven decisions and gain deeper insights into their respective domains. For instance, in healthcare, AI algorithms can assist doctors in diagnosing diseases by analyzing medical records, symptoms, and research data. This not only saves time but also enhances accuracy, leading to better patient outcomes.

Moreover, AI can automate repetitive and mundane tasks, freeing up human resources to focus on more creative and strategic endeavors. By delegating routine tasks to AI systems, individuals can concentrate on problem-solving, innovation, and critical thinking. This shift allows for greater productivity and encourages the exploration of new frontiers.

However, it is important to acknowledge the ethical dimensions of augmenting human capabilities with AI. As we embrace this technology, we must ensure that it is used responsibly and transparently. Safeguards should be in place to prevent biases, protect privacy, and ensure fairness in decision-making processes.

In conclusion, the augmentation of human capabilities with AI holds immense potential for individuals from all walks of life. By harnessing the power of AI, we can unlock new levels of productivity, efficiency, and innovation. However, we must tread carefully, keeping ethics and responsible use at the forefront. With a collaborative approach, AI can truly become a catalyst for transforming data into gold and ushering in a new era of human potential and progress.

The Importance of Human Judgment in AI Decision-Making

In this era of rapid technological advancements and the age of artificial intelligence (AI) alchemy, it is crucial for us to understand the significance of human judgment in AI decision-making. As we delve into the world of AI and witness its transformative power in turning data into gold, it becomes evident that human involvement is essential for ensuring ethical and responsible use of this technology.

AI has undoubtedly revolutionized various industries, from healthcare and finance to transportation and entertainment. Its ability to process massive amounts of data and make predictions based on patterns has enabled us to achieve unprecedented levels of efficiency and accuracy. However, despite its extraordinary capabilities, AI alone cannot possess the moral compass and ethical considerations that humans inherently possess.

One of the key reasons for the importance of human judgment in AI decision-making is the potential for bias in the algorithms. AI systems learn from the data they are trained on, and if this data is biased or flawed, it can lead to biased outcomes. Humans can identify and correct these biases by providing diverse perspectives and scrutinizing the decision-making process. Without human intervention, AI may perpetuate and amplify existing biases, leading to unjust outcomes and reinforcing societal inequalities.

Moreover, human judgment is indispensable in complex decision-making situations where the stakes are high. AI algorithms are designed to optimize specific objectives, but they may not always consider the broader context or long-term consequences. Human judgment can account for intangibles, ethical considerations, and social implications that AI algorithms may overlook. It allows us to make informed decisions that align with our values and consider the impact on individuals and society as a whole.

Furthermore, human judgment is crucial in situations where empathy, creativity, and intuition are required. While AI excels at processing and analyzing vast amounts of data, it lacks the ability to understand emotions, think creatively, or make intuitive leaps. Human judgment can bridge this gap by combining analytical reasoning with emotional intelligence, enabling us to navigate complex situations and make decisions that are empathetic, innovative, and socially responsible.

In conclusion, as we witness the transformative power of AI in the age of AI alchemy, it is imperative to recognize the importance of human judgment in AI decision-making. Human involvement ensures that AI is used ethically, without perpetuating biases or overlooking important considerations. It allows us to make informed decisions, account for intangibles, and navigate complex situations with empathy and creativity. By harnessing the power of AI while relying on human judgment, we can unlock the true potential of this technology and create a future that benefits everyone.

Fostering Trust and Acceptance of AI

In the Age of AI Alchemy: Transforming Data into Gold, the rapid advancements in artificial intelligence (AI) are transforming the way we live, work, and interact with technology. However, for this revolution to truly take hold, it is crucial to foster trust and acceptance of AI among everyone.

Trust is the foundation upon which any technology thrives, and AI is no exception. The public's perception of AI is often colored by misconceptions and fears propagated by sensationalized media stories. To bridge this gap and build trust, it is essential to educate and inform people about the reality of AI.

One way to achieve this is through transparency. Organizations and researchers involved in AI development must be open about their intentions, methodologies, and safeguards in place to address potential concerns. By demystifying the inner workings of AI systems, we can alleviate apprehension and foster trust among individuals.

Ethics also play a crucial role in establishing trust in AI. As AI becomes increasingly integrated into our daily lives, it is vital to ensure that it is developed and deployed in an ethical manner. This means addressing issues such as bias, privacy, and accountability in AI systems. By actively engaging in discussions and debates on ethical considerations, we can create a framework that promotes trust and acceptance of AI.

Furthermore, involving diverse voices in the development and deployment of AI is essential. AI systems should be representative of the societies they serve to avoid biases and ensure fairness. Collaboration between AI experts, policymakers, and individuals from various backgrounds can help create AI systems that are inclusive and trustworthy.

Education is another key aspect of fostering trust and acceptance. By providing accessible and comprehensive information about AI, its capabilities, and limitations, we can empower individuals to make informed decisions and dispel myths. Schools, universities, and community organizations should incorporate AI education into their curricula to equip the next generation with the knowledge and skills needed to navigate the AI-powered world.

Ultimately, fostering trust and acceptance of AI requires collaboration and open dialogue. It is a collective responsibility to ensure that AI is harnessed for the benefit of all. By addressing concerns, promoting transparency, prioritizing ethics, and educating the public, we can build a future where AI is embraced by everyone, transforming data into gold and unlocking its full potential for the betterment of society.

Coexistence and Collaboration in the Age of AI Alchemy

In the era of AI alchemy, where data is transformed into gold, it is crucial for us to understand the importance of coexistence and collaboration. The rapid advancements in technology, particularly in the field of artificial intelligence, have brought about significant changes to our lives and industries. As we navigate this transformative age, it is essential for everyone to recognize the need for harmonious coexistence and collaboration to harness the full potential of AI.

Coexistence refers to the peaceful existence of humans and AI systems in our society. While some may fear that AI will replace human jobs and render us obsolete, the truth is that AI is meant to augment our capabilities, not replace us. The age of AI alchemy presents us with an opportunity to work alongside intelligent machines, leveraging their computational power and analytical abilities to solve complex problems. By embracing coexistence, we can unlock unprecedented levels of productivity and efficiency, paving the way for a future where humans and machines thrive together.

Collaboration, on the other hand, emphasizes the need for cooperation between humans and AI systems. The vast amount of data available today is the fuel that powers AI algorithms. However, this data is not always readily accessible or properly utilized. Collaboration between humans and AI can bridge this gap, allowing us to effectively collect, analyze, and interpret data to make informed decisions. By working hand in hand with AI, we can tap into its ability to process vast amounts of information and gain valuable insights that would otherwise be missed.

The age of AI alchemy offers immense potential for various industries and niches. From healthcare and finance to transportation and entertainment, AI has the power to revolutionize the way we operate. However, to fully embrace this transformation, it is essential for everyone, regardless of their background or expertise, to understand the principles of coexistence and collaboration. This understanding will enable us to navigate the complex world of AI, harnessing its power for the greater good of society.

In conclusion, the subchapter on "Coexistence and Collaboration in the Age of AI Alchemy" emphasizes the importance of peaceful coexistence between humans and AI systems, as well as the need for collaboration to maximize the potential of AI. By embracing coexistence, we can work alongside intelligent machines to unlock unprecedented levels of productivity and efficiency. Collaboration allows us to effectively utilize data and gain valuable insights, propelling various industries forward. In this age of AI alchemy, it is crucial for everyone, regardless of their background, to embrace these principles and actively participate in shaping a future where humans and AI collaborate harmoniously.

Conclusion: Embracing the Alchemy of Data in the AI Revolution

In this book, "AI Revolution: Decoding the Alchemy of Data," we have embarked on a journey to explore the transformative power of artificial intelligence and its ability to turn data into gold. Throughout our exploration, we have witnessed the immense potential of AI alchemy and the possibilities it holds for everyone in the age of AI.

As we have discovered, data is the lifeblood of AI alchemy. It fuels the algorithms that power intelligent systems and enables them to make informed decisions, uncover hidden patterns, and predict future outcomes. In this age of information, data has become an invaluable resource, and those who can harness its power are poised to revolutionize industries, drive innovation, and shape the world around us.

However, it is not enough to simply possess vast amounts of data. To truly unlock its potential, we must embrace the alchemy of data, which involves a careful blend of technology, human expertise, and ethical considerations. AI alchemy is not about replacing humans but augmenting our capabilities, empowering us to make better decisions, and enhancing our problem-solving abilities.

For everyone, regardless of their background or expertise, the age of AI alchemy presents both opportunities and challenges. It offers the chance to tap into new sources of value, whether through personalized recommendations, improved healthcare outcomes, or more efficient business operations. At the same time, it requires us to navigate ethical dilemmas, ensure data privacy, and address the potential biases that can be embedded in AI systems.

To fully embrace the alchemy of data in the AI revolution, we must foster a culture of collaboration, transparency, and continuous learning. As individuals, we should strive to enhance our data literacy, and understanding of the nuances of collecting, analyzing, and interpreting data. As organizations, we should prioritize ethical considerations and invest in the necessary infrastructure and talent to harness the power of AI alchemy responsibly.

The AI revolution is not a distant future; it is happening now, and its impact will only continue to grow. By embracing the alchemy of data, we can not only navigate this revolution but also shape its trajectory for the better. Together, let us embark on this exciting journey and unlock the full potential of AI alchemy in the age of data-driven transformation.

9 788119 747870